52 THINGS TO DO WHILE YOU POO
THE 1980s EDITION

AN HACHETTE UK COMPANY
WWW.HACHETTE.CO.UK

SUMMERSDALE PUBLISHERS LTD
PART OF OCTOPUS PUBLISHING GROUP LIMITED
CARMELITE HOUSE
50 VICTORIA EMBANKMENT
LONDON
EC4Y 0DZ
UK

WWW.SUMMERSDALE.COM
PRINTED AND BOUND IN CHINA
ISBN: 978-1-80007-433-0

SUBSTANTIAL DISCOUNTS ON BULK QUANTITIES OF SUMMERSDALE BOOKS
ARE AVAILABLE TO CORPORATIONS, PROFESSIONAL ASSOCIATIONS AND
OTHER ORGANIZATIONS. FOR DETAILS CONTACT GENERAL ENQUIRIES:
TELEPHONE: +44 (0) 1243 771107 OR EMAIL: ENQUIRIES@SUMMERSDALE.COM.

52 THINGS TO DO WHILE YOU POO

THE 1980s EDITION

HUGH JASSBURN

IF YOU GREW UP IN THE 1980s, YOU KNOW THAT NOTHING COMPARES TO THE MUSIC, FASHION, TOYS, TV, FILMS AND SHEER *FEEL* OF THAT DECADE. BUT HOW MUCH CAN YOU REALLY REMEMBER? WHEN YOU NEXT TAKE A TRIP TO THE TOILET, THIS COLOURFUL COLLECTION OF PUZZLES, ACTIVITIES AND TRIVIA WILL SERVE AS A LEISURELY STROLL DOWN MEMORY LANE, DUSTING OFF HALF-REMEMBERED FACTS AND EVEN FILLING IN A FEW GAPS.

THIS PAIR ONLY APPEARS ONCE
ON THE OPPOSITE PAGE

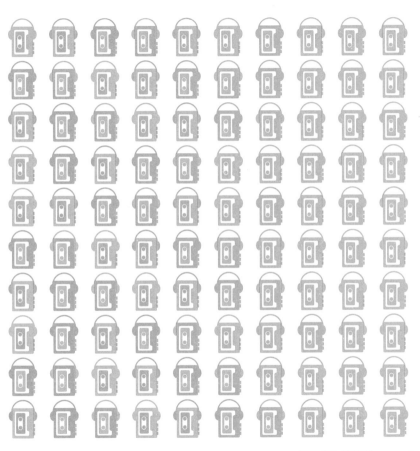

IN 1984, BAND AID RECORDED
"DO THEY KNOW IT'S CHRISTMAS?"
WHO SINGS THE FIRST LINE?

A) GEORGE MICHAEL

B) BOY GEORGE

C) PAUL YOUNG

WWW

TIM BERNERS-LEE IS CREDITED
WITH INVENTING THE WORLD WIDE
WEB IN 1989. WHO WAS HE?

A) AN ENGLISH COMPUTER SCIENTIST

B) AN AMERICAN EVANGELIST

C) A CHINESE ENGINEER

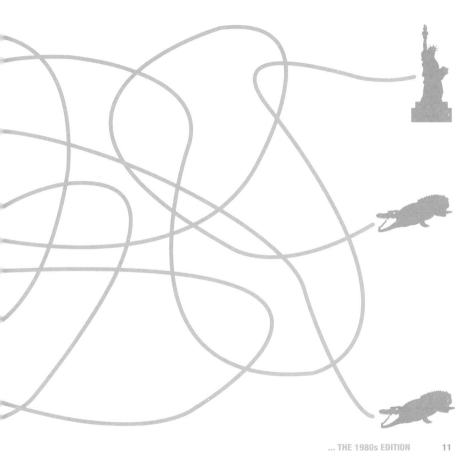

MITTERRAND (FRANÇOIS, PRESIDENT, FRANCE, 81–95)

REAGAN (RONALD, PRESIDENT, USA, 81–89)

THATCHER (MARGARET, PRIME MINISTER, UNITED KINGDOM, 79–90)

GANDHI (INDIRA, PRIME MINISTER, INDIA, 80–84)

ULUSU (BÜLEND, PRIME MINISTER, TURKEY, 80–83)

NAKASONE (YASUHIRO, PRIME MINISTER, JAPAN, 82–87)

SHAMIR (YITZHAK, PRIME MINISTER, ISRAEL, 86–92)

HAWKE (BOB, PRIME MINISTER, AUSTRALIA, 83–91)

LANGE (DAVID, PRIME MINISTER, NEW ZEALAND, 84–89)

MULRONEY (BRIAN, PRIME MINISTER, CANADA, 84–93)

GONZÁLEZ (FELIPE, PRIME MINISTER, SPAIN, 82–96)

M	U	L	R	O	N	E	Y	D	E
X	R	G	A	N	D	H	I	N	R
N	E	O	W	N	A	Y	U	A	T
A	H	N	E	E	G	G	I	R	O
K	C	Z	R	K	C	E	A	R	P
A	T	A	T	W	V	B	U	E	N
S	A	L	Y	A	Z	L	M	T	R
O	H	E	U	H	U	K	J	T	H
N	T	Z	I	S	H	A	M	I	R
E	O	P	U	A	S	D	F	M	G

STRENGTH DOES NOT
COME FROM WINNING.
YOUR STRUGGLES DEVELOP
YOUR STRENGTHS.

ARNOLD SCHWARZENEGGER

THE TERMINATOR NEEDS TO TRAVEL BACK IN TIME!

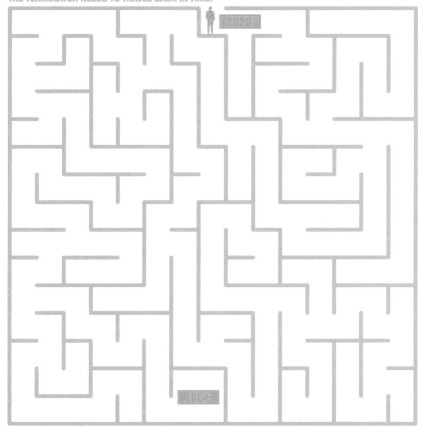

2029

1984

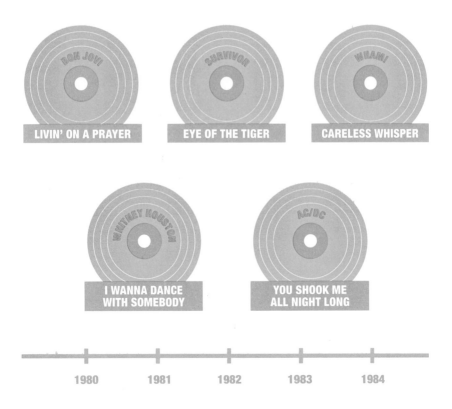

BON JOVI

LIVIN' ON A PRAYER

SURVIVOR

EYE OF THE TIGER

WHAM!

CARELESS WHISPER

WHITNEY HOUSTON

I WANNA DANCE WITH SOMEBODY

AC/DC

YOU SHOOK ME ALL NIGHT LONG

1980   1981   1982   1983   1984

BILLIE JEAN

RED RED WINE

ENDLESS LOVE

WIND BENEATH MY WINGS

WHAT'S LOVE GOT TO DO WITH IT

1985   1986   1987   1988   1989

WHICH CHARACTER APPEARED IN ALL 357 EPISODES OF *DALLAS*?

A) J. R. EWING

B) SUE ELLEN EWING

C) BOBBY EWING

LEG-WARMERS

SHOULDER PADS

HIGH-TOP SNEAKERS

SHELL SUITS

WHICH 1980s FASHION ICON DID THE TV SHOW *FAME* MAKE FAMOUS?

EACH 2x2 BLOCK, COLUMN AND ROW SHOULD CONTAIN THE FOUR 1980s PARTY FAVOURITES

PASTA SALAD

SEX ON THE BEACH

SAUSAGE ON A STICK

MINI BURGERS

THIS PAIR ONLY APPEARS ONCE
ON THE OPPOSITE PAGE

IN 1980, *PAC-MAN* WAS RELEASED.
WHAT WERE THE OTHER CHARACTERS
IN THE MAZE GAME CALLED?

A) BLINKY, PINKY, INKY AND CLYDE

B) PONDY, MONDY, DONDY AND CLOVER

C) STEVE, LEE, PHIL AND CLIVE

WHAT WAS THE FIRST MUSIC VIDEO
TO BE BROADCAST ON MTV WHEN IT WAS
LAUNCHED ON 1 AUGUST 1981?

A) "VIDEO KILLED THE RADIO STAR"
BY THE BUGGLES

B) "MONEY FOR NOTHING" BY DIRE STRAITS

C) "STAND AND DELIVER" BY ADAM ANT

I ONLY WANT TO DO WHAT I REALLY WANT TO DO; OTHERWISE, I'M CONTENT TO SIT HERE AND PLAY MY GUITAR ALL DAY.

EDDIE MURPHY

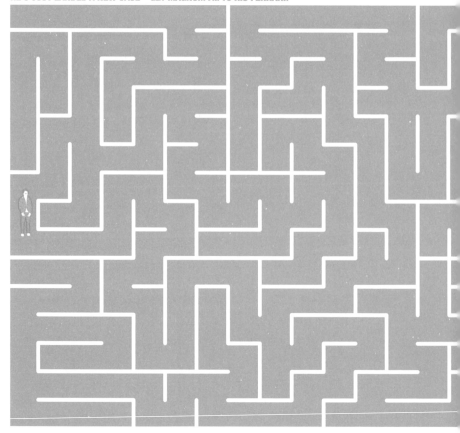

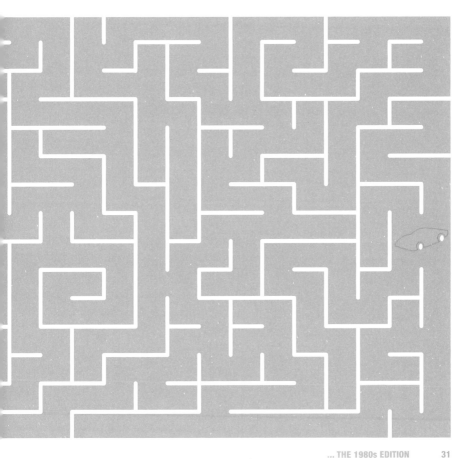

**MADONNA RELEASED HER
DEBUT SINGLE IN OCTOBER 1982.
WHAT WAS IT CALLED?**

A) "EVERYBODY"

B) "LUCKY STAR"

C) "HOLIDAY"

BEFORE CHRISTMAS 1984, 20,000 COUNTERFEITS OF WHICH POPULAR 1980s TOY WERE SEIZED BY CUSTOMS AGENTS?

A) TRANSFORMERS

B) CABBAGE PATCH DOLLS

C) GLO WORMS

RADCLIFFE (DANIEL, 23 JULY, 1989)

CULKIN (MACAULAY, 26 AUGUST 1980)

WILLIAMS (SERENA, 26 SEPTEMBER, 1981)

WINEHOUSE (AMY, 14 SEPTEMBER, 1983)

ADELE (5 MAY, 1988)

EFRON (ZAC, 18 OCTOBER, 1987)

SWIFT (TAYLOR, 13 DECEMBER, 1989)

ZUCKERBERG (MARK, 14 MAY, 1984)

KARDASHIAN (KIM, 21 OCTOBER 1980)

RONALDO (CRISTIANO, 5 FEBRUARY, 1985)

W	G	Z	E	E	L	E	D	A	O
I	C	U	L	K	I	N	E	E	D
L	R	C	T	F	I	W	S	F	L
L	T	K	Y	U	I	N	U	F	A
I	K	E	L	P	O	O	O	I	N
A	Z	R	A	R	D	F	H	L	O
M	L	B	F	H	G	E	E	C	R
S	J	E	K	L	D	Z	N	D	X
K	A	R	D	A	S	H	I	A	N
G	M	G	N	A	Z	B	W	R	C

YOU'RE GOING TO A STEP AEROBICS CLASS –
FIND YOUR SPANDEX!
(FUN FACT: SPANDEX IS AN
ANAGRAM OF EXPANDS!)

EACH 2x2 BLOCK, COLUMN AND ROW SHOULD CONTAIN THE FOUR OBJECTS

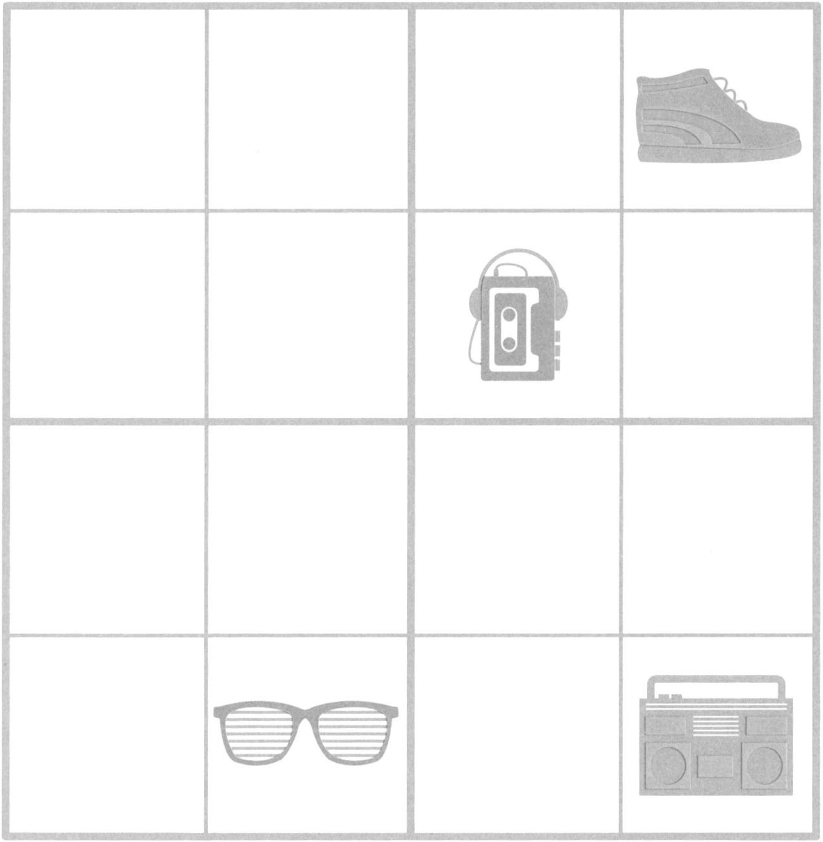

HONESTY IS THE QUALITY
I VALUE MOST IN A FRIEND.
NOT BLUNTNESS, BUT HONESTY
WITH COMPASSION.

BROOKE SHIELDS

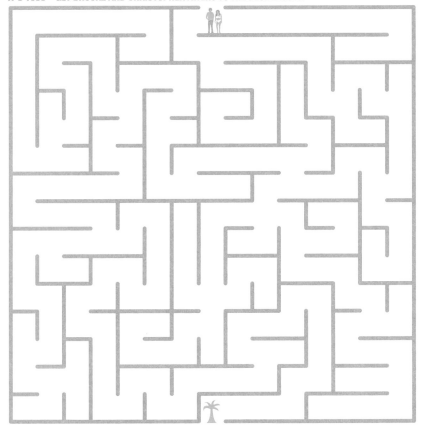

THIS PAIR ONLY APPEARS ONCE
ON THE OPPOSITE PAGE

THE 1980 OLYMPICS WERE
BOYCOTTED BY NEARLY 70 COUNTRIES.
WHERE WAS THE EVENT HELD?

A) MOSCOW

B) SEOUL

C) LOS ANGELES

MICHAEL JACKSON'S 1982 ALBUM
THRILLER IS THE BIGGEST-SELLING ALBUM
OF ALL TIME, BUT WHO PLAYED THE GUITAR
SOLO ON THE TRACK "BEAT IT"?

A) ANGUS YOUNG

B) EDDIE VAN HALEN

C) SLASH

COLOUR THE CUBE!

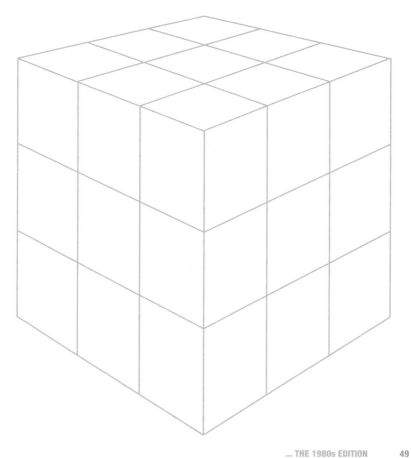

IT'S 29 JULY 1981 AND AN ESTIMATED 750 MILLION PEOPLE HAVE TUNED IN TO WATCH THE ROYAL WEDDING. PRINCE CHARLES HAS LOST THE RING – HELP HIM FIND IT!

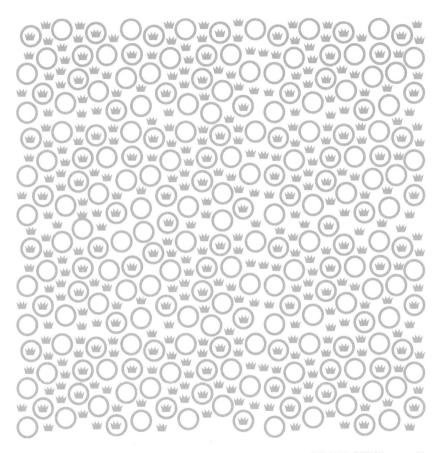

NEVER LET YOUR HEART
TAKE PRECEDENCE OVER REASON,
OTHERWISE YOU WILL
HAVE PROBLEMS.

WHITNEY HOUSTON

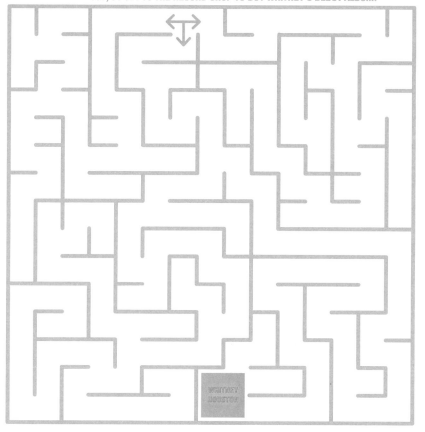

WHO BECAME THE FIRST WESTERN POP
GROUP TO PERFORM IN CHINA ON 7 APRIL
1985, PLAYING A CONCERT IN BEIJING?

A) CULTURE CLUB

B) WHAM!

C) BANANARAMA

IN 1982, HASBRO LAUNCHED SIX MY LITTLE
PONY FIGURINES. WHAT WERE THE
PREVIOUS (RELATIVELY UNSUCCESSFUL)
VERSIONS CALLED?

A) MY PROUD PONY AND PONY BABY

B) MY PRETTY PONY AND BEAUTIFUL BABY

C) MY HAPPY HORSE AND BRIGHT BABY

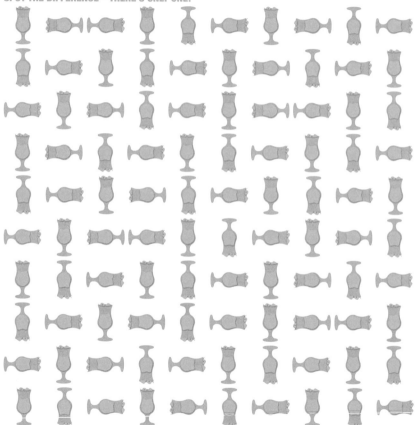

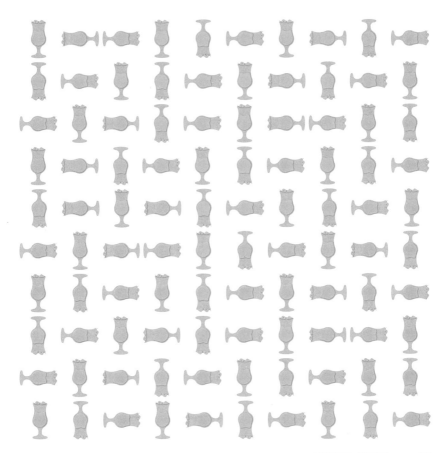

THIS PAIR ONLY APPEARS ONCE
ON THE OPPOSITE PAGE

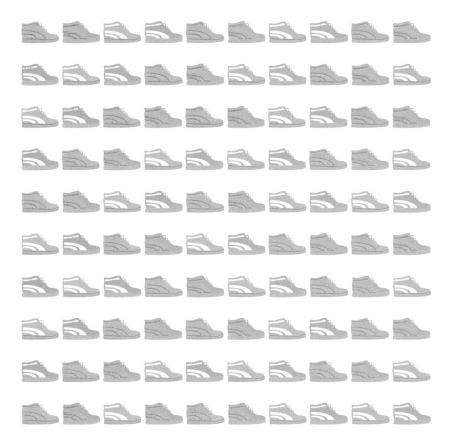

MURPHY (EDDIE)

FOX (MICHAEL J.)

HOGAN (PAUL)

FONDA (JANE)

LAUPER (CYNDI)

HALL (JERRY)

COLLINS (JOAN)

MACCHIO (RALPH)

RUSH (JENNIFER)

NORRIS (CHUCK)

PFEIFFER (MICHELLE)

HAGMAN (LARRY)

```
W  E  R  T  Y  N  U  I  O  M
P  F  N  J  K  A  R  L  U  P
F  X  O  H  G  G  E  R  F  D
E  V  R  N  X  O  P  F  O  X
I  B  R  C  D  H  U  A  I  S
F  N  I  H  Y  A  A  K  H  H
F  M  S  N  I  L  L  O  C  L
E  U  X  W  E  R  T  L  C  C
R  M  N  B  H  A  G  M  A  N
X  U  O  I  E  A  C  V  M  H
```

FIND YOUR "MIX TAPE"

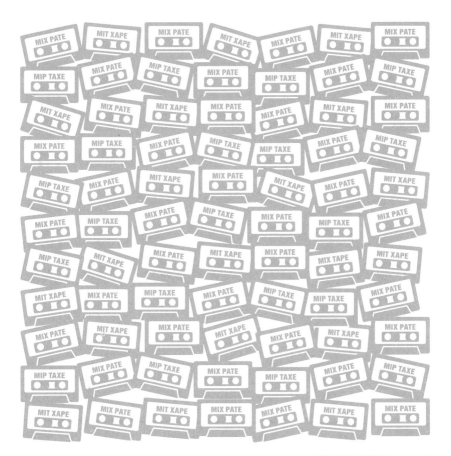

1980s

IN JANUARY 1987, WHO BECAME THE
FIRST WOMAN TO BE INDUCTED INTO
THE ROCK & ROLL HALL OF FAME?

A) TINA TURNER

B) ANNIE LENNOX

C) ARETHA FRANKLIN

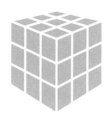

IN 1982, THE FIRST RUBIK'S CUBE
CHAMPIONSHIP WAS WON BY MINH THAI
FROM THE USA, WITH A TIME OF 22.95
SECONDS. WHERE WAS IT HELD?

A) BUDAPEST

B) NEW YORK

C) SYDNEY

EACH 2x2 BLOCK, COLUMN AND ROW SHOULD CONTAIN THE FOUR 1980s HAIRSTYLES

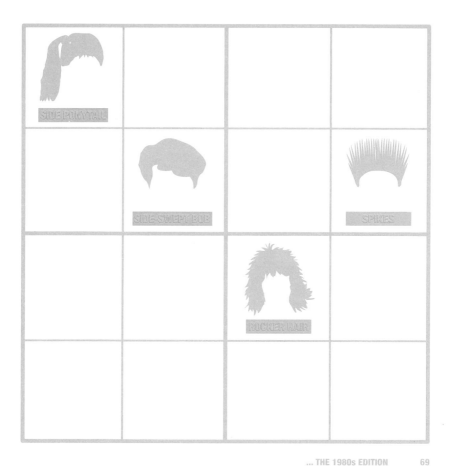

SIDE PONYTAIL

SIDE-SWEPT BOB

SPIKES

ROCKER HAIR

YOU'RE GOING TO A PARTY AND WANT TO CRIMP YOUR HAIR! FIND THE CRIMPERS!

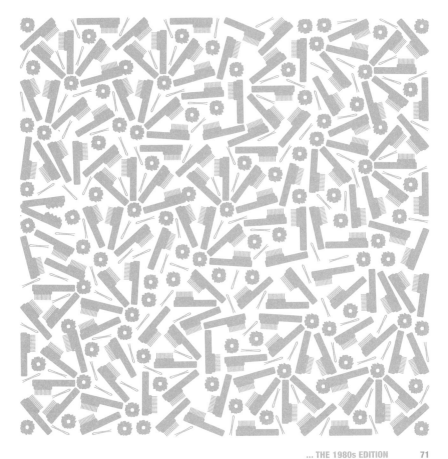

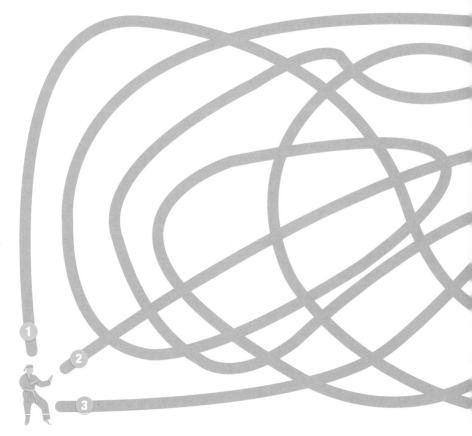

I'M COMPETITIVE.
THAT'S WHAT DEFINES ME,
AND I LOVE IT!

DALEY THOMPSON

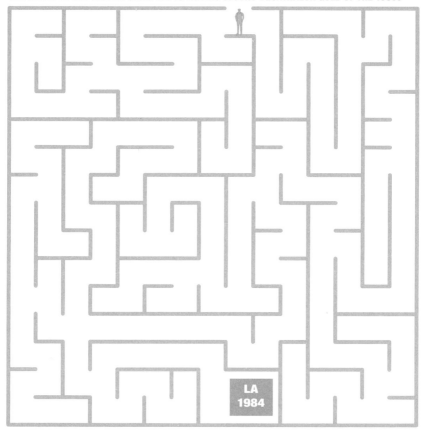

1980 NEW YORK CITY, USA
1980 LOS ANGELES, USA
1981 MIAMI, USA
1982 LA COLLE, MONACO
1982 LOS ANGELES, USA
1983 ILLINOIS, USA
1984 CÉLIGNY, SWITZERLAND
1985 WEST MIDLANDS, ENGLAND
1986 IOWA, USA
1987 NEW YORK CITY, USA
1987 LOS ANGELES, USA
1987 NEW YORK CITY, USA
1989 NEUILLY-SUR-SEINE, FRANCE

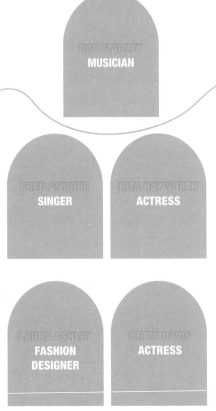

BOB MARLEY
MUSICIAN

FRED ASTAIRE
SINGER

RITA HAYWORTH
ACTRESS

LAURA ASHLEY
FASHION DESIGNER

BETTE DAVIS
ACTRESS

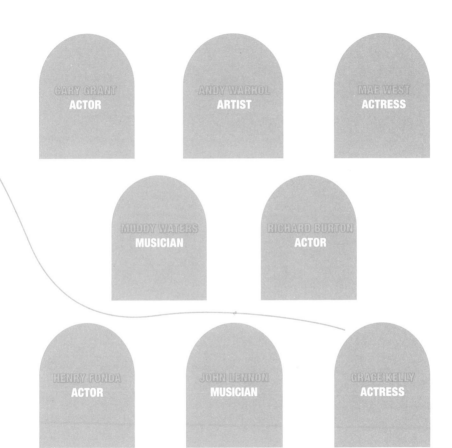

CARY GRANT
ACTOR

ANDY WARHOL
ARTIST

MAE WEST
ACTRESS

MUDDY WATERS
MUSICIAN

RICHARD BURTON
ACTOR

HENRY FONDA
ACTOR

JOHN LENNON
MUSICIAN

GRACE KELLY
ACTRESS

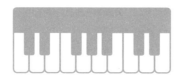

AFTER THE TRAGIC DEATH OF JOY DIVISION FRONTMAN IAN CURTIS IN 1980, WHICH BAND DID THE REMAINING MEMBERS FORM IN 1981?

A) DEPECHE MODE

B) NEW ORDER

C) THE CURE

ON 1 SEPTEMBER 1985, THE WRECK OF WHICH
FAMOUS SHIP WAS DISCOVERED AT A DEPTH
OF ABOUT 3,800 METRES?

A) THE *TITANIC*

B) THE *MARY ROSE*

C) THE *BLACK SWAN*

THIS PAIR ONLY APPEARS ONCE
ON THE OPPOSITE PAGE

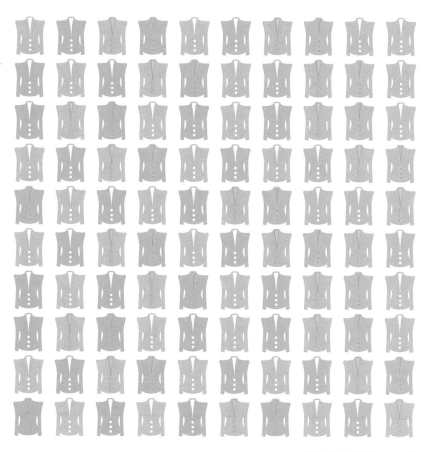

MADONNA

JACKSON (MICHAEL / JANET)

ON THE BLOCK (NEW KIDS)

OSBOURNE (OZZY)

BALLET (SPANDAU)

HOUSTON (WHITNEY)

BLONDIE

POLICE (THE)

ROSES (GUNS N')

MICHAEL (GEORGE)

```
K J A C K S O N E W
C W P L E A H C I M
O E N A P O L I C E
L R O M A D O N N A
B T T S D F G R H J
E Y S E B N U M L K
H G U B L O N D I E
T I O C B L J K L P
N O H S V A A H G F
O R O S E S A B S D
```

ON 19 APRIL 1987, *THE SIMPSONS* MADE THEIR TV DEBUT ON WHICH SHOW?

A) *TOP OF THE POPS*

B) *THE TRACY ULLMAN SHOW*

C) *SESAME STREET*

THE COMPACT DISC, CO-DEVELOPED
BY PHILIPS AND SONY, WAS FIRST
MANUFACTURED IN 1982. WHEN DID MUSIC
CD SALES OVERTAKE TAPE SALES?

A) 1985

B) 1988

C) 1991

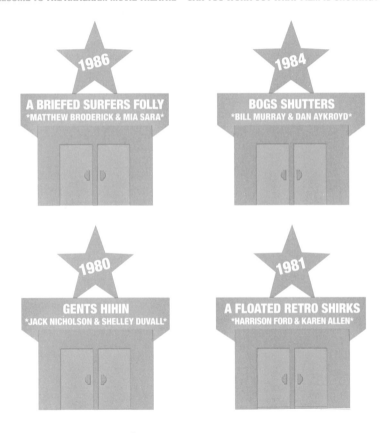

1986

A BRIEFED SURFERS FOLLY
MATTHEW BRODERICK & MIA SARA

1984

BOGS SHUTTERS
BILL MURRAY & DAN AYKROYD

1980

GENTS HIHIN
JACK NICHOLSON & SHELLEY DUVALL

1981

A FLOATED RETRO SHIRKS
HARRISON FORD & KAREN ALLEN

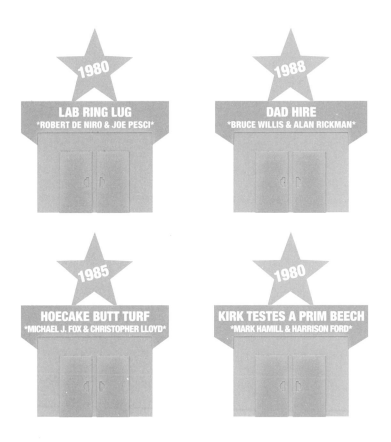

1980
LAB RING LUG
ROBERT DE NIRO & JOE PESCI

1988
DAD HIRE
BRUCE WILLIS & ALAN RICKMAN

1985
HOECAKE BUTT TURF
MICHAEL J. FOX & CHRISTOPHER LLOYD

1980
KIRK TESTES A PRIM BEECH
MARK HAMILL & HARRISON FORD

FIND 1980

1 8 9 0 1 0 9 8 1 8 0 8 1 9 8 9 1 8 0 8
8 1 8 9 0 1 0 9 8 1 8 0 8 1 9 8 9 1 8 0
0 8 1 9 8 9 1 8 0 8 1 8 9 0 1 0 9 8 1 8
8 0 8 1 8 9 0 1 0 9 8 1 8 0 8 1 0 8 9 1
8 1 8 8 0 1 0 9 8 1 8 0 8 1 9 8 9 1 8 0
1 8 9 0 1 0 9 8 1 8 0 8 1 9 8 9 1 8 0 8
8 0 8 1 8 9 0 1 0 9 8 1 8 0 8 1 9 8 9 1
1 8 0 8 1 8 9 0 1 0 9 8 1 8 0 8 1 9 8 9
8 9 0 1 0 9 8 1 8 0 8 1 9 8 9 1 8 0 8 1
1 8 9 0 1 0 9 8 1 8 0 8 1 9 8 9 1 8 0 8
8 1 9 8 9 1 8 0 8 1 8 9 0 1 0 9 8 1 8 0
0 8 1 8 9 0 1 0 9 8 1 8 0 8 1 9 8 9 1 8
1 8 9 0 1 0 9 8 1 8 0 8 1 9 1 9 8 0 0 8
8 9 0 1 0 9 8 1 8 0 8 1 9 8 9 1 8 0 8 1
0 8 1 8 9 0 1 0 9 8 1 8 0 8 1 9 8 9 1 8
8 0 8 1 8 9 0 1 0 9 8 1 8 0 8 1 9 8 9 1
8 9 0 1 9 1 0 1 8 0 8 1 9 8 9 1 8 0 8 1
9 0 1 0 9 8 1 8 0 8 1 9 8 9 1 8 0 8 1 8
8 1 8 9 0 1 0 9 8 1 8 0 8 1 9 8 9 1 8 0
0 8 1 8 9 0 1 0 9 8 1 8 0 8 1 9 8 9 1 8

IN 1988, THE FIRST TRANSATLANTIC FIBRE-OPTIC
CABLE WAS CONSTRUCTED, CARRYING
INFORMATION BETWEEN WHICH COUNTRIES?

A) BRAZIL AND SPAIN

B) USA, UK AND FRANCE

C) CANADA, UK AND FRANCE

WHICH SONG FROM THE SOUNDTRACK OF THE
1986 FILM *TOP GUN* WENT ON TO WIN
AN ACADEMY AWARD?

A) "DANGER ZONE" BY KENNY LOGGINS

B) "TAKE MY BREATH AWAY" BY BERLIN

C) "HOT SUMMER NIGHTS"
BY MIAMI SOUND MACHINE

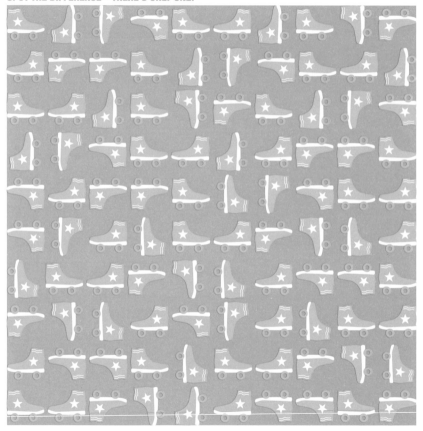

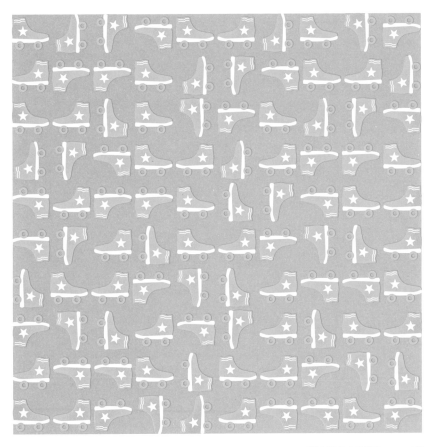

EACH 2x2 BLOCK, COLUMN AND ROW SHOULD CONTAIN THE FOUR 1980s TOYS

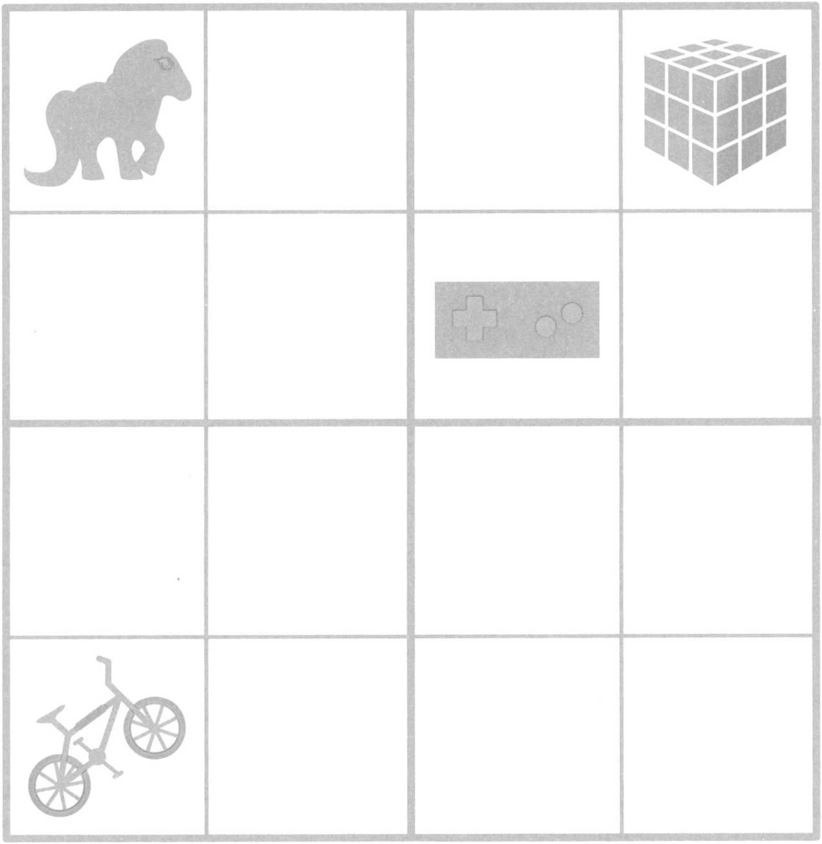

ON 1 OCTOBER 1982, DISNEY OPENED THE EPCOT
THEME PARK. WHAT DOES EPCOT STAND FOR?

A) ENTERTAINMENT PLAY
COMMUNITY OF TOMORROW

B) END PLAY: COMMENCE OWN TEACHING

C) EXPERIMENTAL PROTOTYPE
COMMUNITY OF TOMORROW

ON 21 APRIL 1989, NINTENDO RELEASED
THE PORTABLE GAME BOY. WHAT WAS ONE
OF THE LAUNCH GAMES?

A) *POKÉMON*

B) *DONKEY KONG*

C) *SUPER MARIO LAND*

LA LADS

RED RING KITH

HEAT MEAT

GLACE CANDY YEN

SLIGHTED LONGER

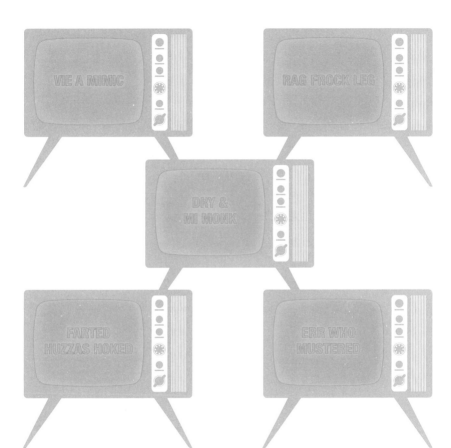

VIE A MIMIC

RAG FROCK LEG

DRY &
MI MONK

FARTED
HUZZAS HOKED

ERR WHO
MUSTERED

P6–7

P12–13

P8 C) PAUL YOUNG
P9 A) AN ENGLISH COMPUTER SCIENTIST
P10–11

P15

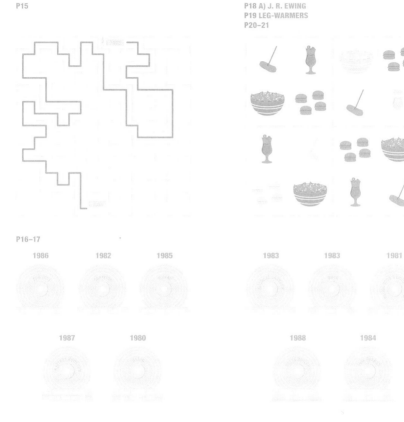

P16–17

1986   1982   1985

1983   1983   1981

1987   1980

1988   1984

P22–23

P29

P24 A) BLINKY, PINKY, INKY AND CLYDE
P25 A) "VIDEO KILLED THE RADIO STAR" BY THE BUGGLES
P26–27

P30–31

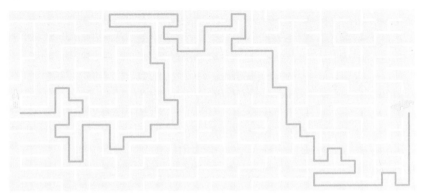

P32 A) "EVERYBODY"
P33 B) CABBAGE PATCH DOLLS
P34–35

P36–37

P38–39

P42–43

P41

P44–45

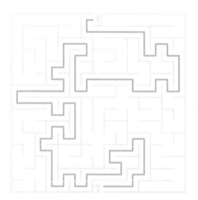

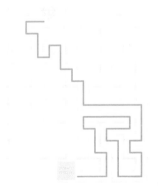

P60–61

P62–63

P64–65

P66 C) ARETHA FRANKLIN
P67 A) BUDAPEST
P68–69

P70–71

P75

P72–73

BOB MARLEY
1981
MIAMI, USA

CARY GRANT
1986
IOWA, USA

ANDY WARHOL
1987
NEW YORK CITY
USA

MAE WEST
1980
LOS ANGELES
USA

FRED ASTAIRE
1987
LOS ANGELES
USA

RITA HAYWORTH
1987
NEW YORK CITY
USA

MUDDY WATERS
1983
ILLINOIS, USA

RICHARD BURTON
1984
CÉLIGNY
SWITZERLAND

LAURA ASHLEY
1985
WEST MIDLANDS
ENGLAND

BETTE DAVIS
1989
NEUILLY-SUR-
SEINE, FRANCE

HENRY FONDA
1982
LOS ANGELES
USA

JOHN LENNON
1980
NEW YORK CITY
USA

GRACE KELLY
1982
LA COLLE
MONACO

P78 B) NEW ORDER
P79 A) THE *TITANIC*
P80–81

P82–83

K J A C K S O N E W
C W P L E A H C I M
O E N A P O L I C E
L R O M A D O N N A
B T T S D F C R H J
E Y S E B N U M L K
H G U B L O N D I E
T I O C B L I K L P
N O H S V A H G F
O R O S E S B S D

P84 B) *THE TRACY ULLMAN SHOW*
P85 C) 1991
P86–87

FERRIS BUELLER'S DAY OFF

GHOSTBUSTERS

RAGING BULL

DIE HARD

THE SHINING

RAIDERS OF THE LOST ARK

BACK TO THE FUTURE

THE EMPIRE STRIKES BACK

P90 B) USA, UK AND FRANCE
P91 B) "TAKE MY BREATH AWAY" BY BERLIN
P92–93

P88–89

1 9 8 0

ALSO BY HUGH JASSBURN

52 THINGS TO DO WHILE YOU POO

52 THINGS TO LEARN ON THE LOO

52 THINGS TO DOODLE WHILE YOU POO

52 THINGS TO DO WHILE YOU POO
THE FART EDITION

52 THINGS TO DO WHILE YOU POO
THE TURD EDITION

52 THINGS TO DO WHILE YOU POO
THE SPORTS EDITION

52 THINGS TO DO WHILE YOU POO
THE RUGBY PUZZLE BOOK

52 THINGS TO DO WHILE YOU POO
THE FOOTBALL PUZZLE BOOK

52 THINGS TO DO WHILE YOU POO
THE CRICKET PUZZLE BOOK

52 THINGS TO DO WHILE YOU POO
NOT THE BOG STANDARD EDITION

52 THINGS TO DO WHILE YOU POO
HUNT THE DUMP

52 THINGS TO DO WHILE YOU POO
THE 1960s EDITION

52 THINGS TO DO WHILE YOU POO
THE 1970s EDITION

HAVE YOU ENJOYED THIS BOOK? IF SO, FIND US ON FACEBOOK AT SUMMERSDALE PUBLISHERS, ON TWITTER AT @SUMMERSDALE AND ON INSTAGRAM AT @SUMMERSDALEBOOKS AND GET IN TOUCH. WE'D LOVE TO HEAR FROM YOU!

WWW.SUMMERSDALE.COM